A Student's Guide to

Writer's Help

A Bedford/St. Martin's Online Handbook

D1272621

A Student's Guide to
Writer's Help
A Bedford/St. Martin's Online Handbook

Stephen A. Bernhardt
University of Delaware

BEDFORD/ST. MARTIN'S   Boston ◆ New York

Contents

Introduction

Got a question about writing?

Open *Writer's Help,* and you'll find fast, reliable, up-to-date advice, even when you aren't sure how to ask your question. Not all writers know exactly what they're looking for. So we talked to 1,600 college students from across the country and then used what we heard to build a search engine that works better for writers, with targeted results that are easy to navigate.

You already know how to use a simple search engine. And you probably know how to tag and save your favorite photographs or videos. *Writer's Help* is based on these familiar online tools, so you can easily find and save clear examples and explanations that will help you become a better writer.

What do you want to know? Ask *Writer's Help,* a handbook unlike any other.

Getting started

Check system requirements.

Windows systems: Windows 2000, XP SP1, XP SP2, Vista
                              Internet Explorer 6, 7
                              Firefox 1.0.7+

Mac systems: Mac OS 10.2+
                              Firefox 1.0.7+
                              Safari 1.2+

Register an activation code.

If this student guide includes a 16-character activation code inside the front cover, complete the steps below. (If you do not have an activation code, skip to p. 4 for purchase instructions.)

1. Point your browser to http://writershelp.com.

2. Click on "Enter your activation code."

3. In the pop-up window that appears, enter the activation code exactly as it is printed inside the front cover of this booklet.

4. Enter your first name, your last name, your e-mail address, and your instructor's e-mail address in the text fields. (Entering your instructor's e-mail address allows you to view any tags, notes, or new content your instructor adds for your class.) Create a password and password hint.

5. Click on the "Next" button and confirm your account information.

You are now registered. When you visit *Writer's Help,* you can log in with your e-mail address and password; you will not need the activation code again.

Contact technical support for help:
    Call 1-800-936-6899.
    Go to http://bfwpub.com/techsupport.

Writer's Help
Diana Hacker ○ Stephen A. Bernhardt ○ Nancy Sommers

A **Bedford/St. Martin's**
Online Handbook

Learn More ▽   Instructors ▽   Students ▽   Training & Support ▽

Who's into **Writer's Help**?*
*since September 2010

15,662 instructors   **5,589** students   **1,926,023** pages viewed

Learn More ▶

Log in

E-mail address

Password

Log in   Forgot your password?

Students:
Enter your activation code >
Purchase access >

Instructors:
Request instructor access >

Enter your activation code >

Real students. **1,600 of them.**

A college writer's handbook—
reimagined
What's the buzz? Find out ▶

Register an Activation Code

● Enter the following information to register your copy of Writer's Help e-Book:

Activation Code * :

First Name:

Last Name:

Email:

Note: Your e-mail address will serve as your username for the e-Book.

» Please enter a **password** for your account. Your password must be between 4 and 20 characters long, and may contain only letters, numbers, and/or the underscore ("_") character. (If you've previously registered for any other website associated with a Bedford/St. Martins, W.H. Freeman, or Worth Publishers textbook, use the same password you used then. If you're not sure, just enter a password below and we'll check it for you.)

Password:

Retype Password:

» Optional: Enter a question that will remind you of your password, should you forget it. For example, if your password is a street address, your hint might be: Where did I live when I was 12?

Password Hint:

» Enter your instructor's e-mail address. This is required for submitting results from quizzes and other exercises to your instructor. If you are not sure you need your instructor's e-mail address or don't know it, you can leave the field blank and provide this information on another visit.

Instructor's E-mail:

Purchase access.

If this student guide does not include a 16-character activation code inside the front cover, complete the steps below. (If you do have an activation code, turn to p. 2 for registration instructions.)

1. Point your browser to http://writershelp.com.

2. Click on the "Purchase access" link.

3. In the pop-up window that appears, select a 2-year or 4-year subscription. Indicate whether you are in a college or university or a high school. Enter the zip code of your college, university, or high school. Click "Next."

4. In the next window, enter your first name, your last name, your e-mail address, and your instructor's e-mail address in the text fields. (Entering your instructor's e-mail address allows you to view any tags, notes, or new content your instructor adds for your class.) Create a password and password hint. Select your school from the pull-down menu. Click on the "Next" button.

5. Enter your payment information, including your name (as it appears on your credit card), your credit card number and expiration date, and your billing address.

6. Click on the "Next" button. After confirming your information, click on the "Place your order" button.

You now have access. When you visit *Writer's Help* again, you can log in with your e-mail address and password.

Contact technical support for help:
Call 1-800-936-6899.
Go to http://bfwpub.com/techsupport.

Writer's Help

Diana Hacker ○ Stephen A. Bernhardt ○ Nancy Sommers

A **Bedford/St. Martin's**
Online Handbook

Product Information -> Account Information -> Payment Information -> Confirm -> Receipt

Purchase Access

You are about to purchase access to **Writer's Help**.

Each subscription is for the sole use of the original purchaser, and cannot be shared or transferred.

Select the version of this e-Handbook you'd like to purchase:
- ◉ A 2-year subscription to the standard version (all chapters) of the e-Handbook ($31.95)
- ○ A 4-year subscription to the standard version (all chapters) of the e-Handbook ($37.95)

Is the course for which you are using the e-Handbook being offered by a...
◉ college or university   or   ○ high school?

Please enter the zip code or postal code
of your **college, university, or high school:** [   ]
(If you do not know the zip code or postal code of your school, enter your home zip code or postal code.)

NEXT ▶

If you experience difficulties with this purchasing process please call our toll-free technical support number (800) 936-6899, available from 9:00 A.M. to 3:00 A.M., Eastern Time, Monday through Friday and 11:30 A.M. to 8:00 P.M. Eastern Time, Saturday and Sunday. You may also reach us via e-mail at **techsupport@bfwpub.com**, or visit us at **http://bfwpub.com/techsupport**.

Get your bearings.

Once you're logged in, you'll see all three panels of *Writer's Help.*

In the center is the search bar and the "Getting started" (home) page. If your instructor has assigned material in *Writer's Help,* you will see a list of assignments on the home page.

The left panel, where your search results will display, is also where you'll find the table of contents, the index, a list of interactive exercises, and a scorecard that keeps track of your exercise results.

The right panel is where you'll find tags, notes, highlighting, and page-sharing options. In this panel, you can also change your user settings, view class tags, and see trends in tagging and searching. Clicking on "About Writer's Help" will take you to additional support for using the site.

Writer's Help is designed to work side-by-side with other applications you are using, so you can reduce its size by closing the side panels. If you want to view only the center panel, click on "Close navigation" to close the left panel and "Close tags, tools & help" to close the right. (You may need to resize your browser window to view other applications along with *Writer's Help.*)

Finding help

Search for advice.

You can get into *Writer's Help* quickly by searching.

To begin, type your term in the search bar in the center panel and click on the "search" button.

Your search can take many forms. Here are just a few ways you can express what you're looking for:

- as a single word, such as *fragment*
- as a phrase, such as *MLA paper format*
- as a question, such as *Does a period go inside the quotation marks?*

When you click the "search" button, search results will display in the left panel. Results are sorted into topic categories that can be expanded or collapsed. The number in parentheses shows how many results are in each category. Clicking on a search result launches new content in the center panel or opens a pop-up window.

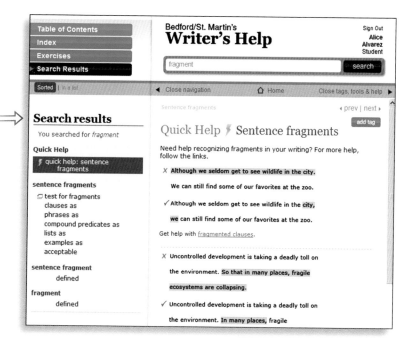

Check out other tips and tools.

If you still don't see what you're looking for, you can

- try another search. If you can't think of a particular term, try to describe the problem. If you can't remember *thesis,* for example, try typing in *main idea* or *main point.*

- try a suggestion from the search tips on the *Writer's Help* "Getting started" page (click on the "Home" button below the search bar)

- return to the home page to check your instructor's assigned tags for ideas (see pp. 18–19)

- click on a "related search" term at the end of a search results list

You can also

- browse the table of contents. The list of topics lets you see everything that's available and it might help you pinpoint what you're looking for.

- browse the index

Use Quick Help.

Quick Help pages show you advice at a glance with a series of examples. You can skim the examples to get an answer quickly and get back to your writing. If you need more help or want to know more about a topic, just follow the blue underlined links to fuller explanations.

You can find Quick Help pages

- by looking for the lightning bolt icon in a list of search results or in the table of contents

- by entering *quick help* in the search bar to get a list of all Quick Help pages

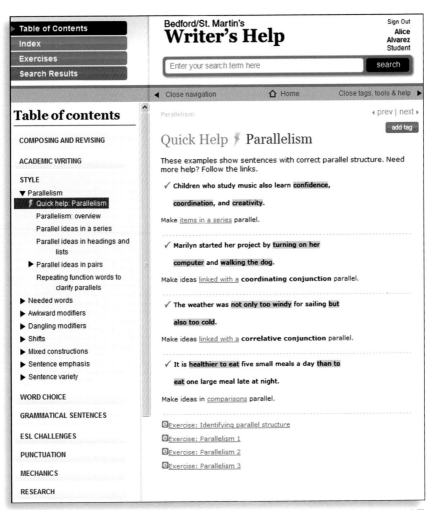

Bedford/St. Martin's
Writer's Help

Enter your search term here   search

◀ Close navigation   ⌂ Home   Close tags, tools & help ▶

Table of contents

Parallelism   ◀ prev | next ▶

add tag

Quick Help ⚡ Parallelism

These examples show sentences with correct parallel structure. Need more help? Follow the links.

✓ Children who study music also learn **confidence**, **coordination**, and **creativity**.

Make items in a series parallel.

✓ Marilyn started her project by **turning on her computer** and **walking the dog**.

Make ideas linked with a **coordinating conjunction** parallel.

✓ The weather was **not only too windy** for sailing **but also too cold**.

Make ideas linked with a **correlative conjunction** parallel.

✓ It is **healthier to eat** five small meals a day **than to eat** one large meal late at night.

Make ideas in comparisons parallel.

Exercise: Identifying parallel structure
Exercise: Parallelism 1
Exercise: Parallelism 2
Exercise: Parallelism 3

Personalizing and sharing

Tag your favorite pages.

Tagging is a way of saving your favorite pages. When you find helpful pages that you'll want to revisit easily, you can tag them with your own terms. Just click the "add tag" button in the upper right corner of the page you want to save. Enter the term you want to associate with the page and click "save." (If you want your tag to apply to surrounding pages as well, check the box for "Tag the whole section.")

You might want to tag pages that help with a particular writing challenge or with a specific assignment. For instance, you might apply the tag *main idea* to several different pages that are especially helpful when you're working with thesis statements.

You can also think of tagging as a way of personalizing your search results. When you type one of your own tags in the search bar, all the pages associated with that tag will show up at the top of your list of search results. You can also search on a tag by clicking on it in the "Your Tags" list in the Tags and Tools tab in the right panel (for more about this list, see p. 16).

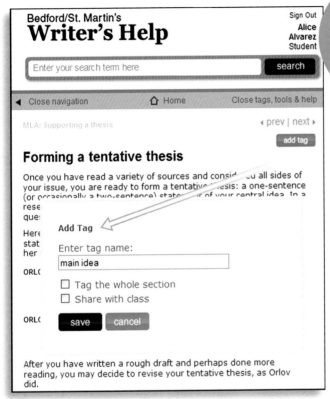

Bedford/St. Martin's
Writer's Help

Sign Out
Alice
Alvarez
Student

Enter your search term here | **search**

◄ Close navigation   ⌂ Home   Close tags, tools & help

MLA: Supporting a thesis   ◄ prev | next ►

add tag

Forming a tentative thesis

Once you have read a variety of sources and consid___ __u all sides of
your issue, you are ready to form a tentativ___ __esis: a one-sentence
(or occasionally a two-sentence) state___ __ of your central idea. In a
rese
que:

Here
stat
her

ORL(

ORL(

Add Tag ◄

Enter tag name:

main idea

☐ Tag the whole section
☐ Share with class

save   cancel

After you have written a rough draft and perhaps done more
reading, you may decide to revise your tentative thesis, as Orlov
did.

To start tagging,
click the add tag
button in the upper
right corner of
the page you want
to save.

Manage your tags.

You can view your list of tags at any time to edit the list or see your saved pages. Just click on "Open tags, tools & help" under the search bar to open the right panel, and select the "Tags and Tools" tab.

To change the name of a tag, roll over it and click on the word "edit." The tag will appear in the edit box, where you can make changes. When a tag is no longer useful, you can delete it.

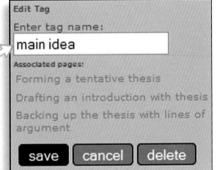

About Writer's Help

Tags and Tools

Your Class

Top Ten

Add a tag

- Your Tags

You have no tags for this page.

Your tags for all pages: VIEW AS CLOUD

Approaching assignments
Approaching assignments in the disciplines

MLA
Directory to MLA works cited models (MLA PAPERS)

calendar
Sample schedule for a research paper

main idea edit
Forming a tentative thesis
Drafting an introduction with thesis
Backing up the thesis with lines of argument

- Recently viewed pages

- Share a link

- Your Notes

- Highlight

- Settings

- Update account

- Scorecard

Edit Tag

Enter tag name:

main idea

Associated pages:
Forming a tentative thesis
Drafting an introduction with thesis
Backing up the thesis with lines of argument

save   cancel   delete

View tags from your instructor.

If you entered your instructor's e-mail address when you registered with *Writer's Help* (see p. 2 or 4), you can see and search by tags that your instructor has saved for your class. Every time you log in, the pages your instructor has tagged as assignments will appear on the "Getting started" page. If you navigate away from this page and want to return to this list of tags from your instructor, just click the "Home" icon below the search bar.

Bedford/St. Martin's
Writer's Help

Enter your search term here   search

◀ Close navigation   ⌂ Home   Close tags, tools & help ▶

‹ prev | next ›

add tag

Getting started

Enter a word or phrase in the search box above.

See a list of search tips.

Browse a list of suggested searches.

Need more help?

Read A Student's Guide to *Writer's Help*.

Contact tech support.

Contact the editors.

View assigned pages:

in-class activity: writing paragraphs
Writing an introduction
Placing the thesis statement in the introduction
Drafting the body
Drafting a conclusion
Paragraph patterns
Paragraph coherence
Providing a hook in your introduction

Share tags with your class.

You and your classmates share a set of class tags so that you can refer each other to useful pages. To see the class tags, click the "Your Class" tab at the top of the right panel.

To share a tag with your class, find the page you want to tag. Then click the "add tag" button on that page. Type the tag you'd like to associate with that page, and click on the checkbox next to the "Share with class" option.

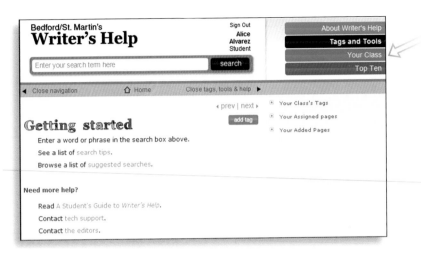

Bedford/St. Martin's
Writer's Help

Sign Out
Alice Alvarez
Student

About Writer's Help
Tags and Tools
Your Class
Top Ten

Enter your search term here   **search**

◄ Close navigation   ⌂ Home   Close tags, tools & help ►

◄ prev | next ►

add tag

⊛ Your Class's Tags
⊛ Your Assigned pages
⊛ Your Added Pages

Getting started

Enter a word or phrase in the search box above.

See a list of search tips.

Browse a list of suggested searches.

Need more help?

Read A Student's Guide to *Writer's Help*.

Contact tech support.

Contact the editors.

Add Tag

Enter tag name:

☐ Tag the whole section
☐ Share with class

save   cancel

Find out what other students search for and save.

The right panel is where you'll personalize the product (with tags, notes, highlighting, and user settings) and find out how other writers are working with *Writer's Help*.

If the right panel is closed, click on "Open tags, tools & help" under the search bar to open it. Clicking on the tab "Top Ten" in the right panel will take you to lists of popular tags and recent tags. These lists reflect how users of this product across the country refer to the help they find.

You can click on any of the tags to run a search and see what pages other users are associating with that tag. If you like the tag and the results associated with it, you can adopt the tag. The word "adopt" appears next to each tag when you roll over the tag.

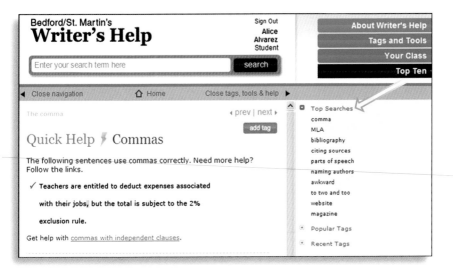

Model student papers in *Writer's Help*

The model papers and other sample documents in *Writer's Help* represent various genres (or types) of academic writing in five different citation styles. Each paper includes annotations that teach lessons about formatting and good writing. In this list the citation style is given in parentheses following each title.

Analysis (of texts and visuals)

Lee, "The Golden Arches Go Green: McDonald's and Real Lettuce" (MLA)

Lopez, " 'A Question of Ethics' Left Unanswered" (MLA)

Sanchez, "Rethinking Big-Box Stores" (MLA)

Analysis (of literary works)

Larson, "The Transformation of Mrs. Peters: An Analysis of 'A Jury of Her Peers' " (MLA)

Peel, "Opposing Voices in 'Ballad of the Landlord' " (MLA)

Annotated Bibliography

Haddad, "Patterns of Gender-Related Differences in Online Communication: An Annotated Bibliography" (APA)

Orlov, "Online Monitoring: A Threat to Employee Privacy in the Wired Workplace: An Annotated Bibliography" (MLA)

Argument

Hammond, "Performance Enhancement through Biotechnology Has No Place in Sports" (MLA)

Jacobs, "From Lecture to Conversation: Redefining What's 'Fit to Print' " (MLA)

Lund, "Preserving Yellowstone's Winter Wilderness" (MLA)

Sanghvi, "Preserving Winter Access: Snowmobiles in Yellowstone National Park" (MLA)

Watson, "Hooked on Credit Cards" (MLA)

Zhang, "Slow Down and Eat Better" (MLA)

Clinical Practice

Riss, "Acute Lymphoblastic Leukemia and Hypertension in One Client: A Nursing Practice Paper" (APA)

Draft/Paper-in-Progress

Watson, "Hooked on Credit Cards" (MLA)

Zhang, "The Importance of Food" (MLA)

Lab Report

Johnson and Arnold, "Distribution Pattern of Dandelion (*Taraxacum officinale*) on an Abandoned Golf Course" (CSE)

Literature Review

Charat, "Always Out of Their Seats (and Fighting): Why Are Boys Diagnosed with ADHD More Often Than Girls?" (APA)

Martin, "Hypothermia, the Diving Reflex, and Survival" (CSE)

Memo

Business memo

Outline

Levi, "Cell Phones in the Hands of Drivers: A Risk or a Benefit?" (MLA)

Orlov, "Online Monitoring: A Threat to Employee Privacy in the Wired Workplace" (MLA)

Proposal

O'Bryan, "Site Stabilization Plan for Erosion Control" (USGS)

Ratajczak, "Proposal to Add a Wellness Program" (APA)

Reflective Essay

Gibson, "A Reflection on Service Learning: Working with Eric" (APA)

Reflective Letter

Bonilla, Portfolio Cover Letter

Report

Spencer, "Positively Affecting Employee Morale" (APA)

Thompson, "Crime in Leesburg, Virginia" (APA)

Research Essay

Benjamin, "Wage Slavery or True Independence? Women Workers in the Lowell, Massachusetts, Textile Mills, 1820-1850" (*Chicago*)

Bishop, "The Massacre at Fort Pillow: Holding Nathan Bedford Forrest Accountable" (*Chicago*)

Daly, "A Call to Action: Regulate Use of Cell Phones on the Road" (MLA)

Levi, "Cell Phones in the Hands of Drivers: A Risk or a Benefit?" (MLA)

Mirano, "Can Medication Cure Obesity in Children? A Review of the Literature" (APA)

Orlov, "Online Monitoring: A Threat to Employee Privacy in the Wired Workplace" (MLA)

Résumé

Traditional résumé

Scannable résumé

Web résumé

Review

Houston, "Concert Review: Cincinnati Symphony Orchestra" (MLA)